YOUR KIDS *and* ROCK

BOB LARSON

POCKET GUIDES
Tyndale House Publishers, Inc.
Wheaton, Illinois

Readers may write to the author at the following address:

Bob Larson
P.O. Box 36480
Denver, CO 80236

Your Kids and Rock is adapted from *Larson's Book of Rock*, copyright 1987 by Bob Larson.

First printing, November 1988
Library of Congress Catalog Card Number 88-50920
ISBN 0-8423-8611-4

Printed in the United States of America

CONTENTS

INTRODUCTION

The Beat Goes On

You're reading a book in the den. You try to ignore the booming beat upstairs. Why can't your daughter listen to soft, soothing music, the kind you enjoy? It would prepare her mind better to do algebra equations.

Laying your book down, you head for your daughter's bedroom, up the stairs and to the door. No need to worry that she'll hear you coming.

You open the door. She's seated at the desk with her back to you. Bouncing up and down in the chair, she occasionally uses her pencil. She is doing homework, but you'll never know how. There's the stereo, and there's the plug. Pull it, and tranquility will be restored to your home.

But does pulling that plug mean your daughter won't listen to rock music elsewhere? Definitely not.

Remember, you allowed those records in your home in the first place. What if your heavy disciplinary hand creates rebellion rather than submission? Wouldn't it be wiser to find out why your daughter likes that music? You need to understand the appeal of the beat, and you need to understand names and terminology. When you discuss music, teenagers become defensive. They're looking for semantic blunders to negate your opinions of their musical tastes. Calling Phil Collins hard rock (he's not) or assuming that every group lays down primitive, unsophisticated beat patterns (Journey does not) may be the mortal sin that shuts down communication.

IS IT "ROCK" OR "ROCK 'N' ROLL"?

Many parents are confused about "rock" versus "rock 'n' roll." The term *rock* is an abbreviation of *rock 'n' roll,* but a chronological and musical distinction between these terms has evolved. Though both are used interchangeably, *rock 'n' roll* more precisely refers to pre-1964 sounds or present-day music that emulates the music of artists like Little Richard, Elvis, Bill Haley, Chuck Berry, and the early Beach Boys. It was played mainly by blacks who used pianos and horns, whereas today's rock 'n' roll is primarily performed by white bands with guitars and drums predominating.

The broadened term *rock* came into journalistic vogue in the late sixties and refers to post-Beatle music. Its definition is less precise and may include the work of such diverse artists as Billy Joel and Eric Clapton. As the product of self-aware musicians, rock is more middle-class than its predecessor, but the terms *rock* and *rock 'n' roll* are used interchangeably by musicians and the record-buying public.

THE BEAT'S THE THING

One thing can't be overemphasized: *The focus of rock is the beat*. Despite variations and transitions, rock's essential beat survived. Whatever harmonic, melodic, or verbal sophistication rock may contain, its appeal is its simple, rhythmic, pounding beat.

An incessantly driving, pulsated beat pattern is not inherently evil, but when applied for a protracted period of time at high volume, it can be hypnotic at live concerts. Like any repetitious assault on one's neurosensory apparatus, it can shut down conscious mental processes. This is the same technique used in Eastern meditative disciplines, like Transcendental Meditation. The result is a heightened suggestibility to images and messages. Rock audiences can be almost hypnotized by the performers, and if the performers are conveying such messages as "Sex is everything," "Down with authority," or "Life is meaningless, so have fun and die young," audiences can be amazingly receptive. Adults with an ingrained value system might not be affected at all by a rock show, but children and teens are fair game for any message pounded home with a driving beat.

Do you understand now why your child is so caught up in the beat? It's not just noise. It's a carefully constructed rhythm captivating their bodies and capturing their minds. Because of the high-energy world in which you are raising them, they have developed a physiological affinity for the beat.

You must understand that driving sound for how it envelopes your child's world. He moves to the sound of a different drummer, and no matter how much you detest it, he likes it. Don't mock it or knock it. That won't get you anywhere.

The beat, you see, isn't the real problem. But the beat can often serve to introduce listeners to a world where sex becomes mere recreation, drugs and alcohol are used with abandon, and cult and occult practices are promoted. No, all songs and all performers are not out to destroy America's morals. But before we examine what you, as a parent, can do about your child and rock, let's look at some people whose lyrics and life-styles are morally questionable.

CHAPTER

1

The Sexual Party in Rock

In 1954, Cleveland disc jockey Alan Freed was searching for a term to describe teenagers' wild response to a new musical fad. Freed found his phrase in a ghetto expression for fornication: rock 'n' roll. The name stuck, and the beat went on. Rock lyrics eventually explored fringes of lyrical porn Freed never dreamed of.

Love means sex to most contemporary rock composers. If meaningful relationships are referred to at all, they usually are described as fruitless or pointlessly painful. Most rock expresses love in a single dimension–desire. Lust is the motivation, conquest the goal.

Many song titles in the last several years seem to extol premarital and extramarital sex. Consider George Michael's "I Want Your Sex" and Marvin Gaye's "Sexual Healing." Ray Parker, Jr.'s "The Other Woman" and Whitney Houston's "Saving All My Love for You" made adultery sound delightful.

Album titles aren't exactly mild, either. Some that come to mind are Poison's *Open Up and Say Ahh*, Wham's *Make It Big,* Tina Turner's *Break Every Rule,* David Lee Roth's *Eat 'Em and Smile,* Ratt's *Dancing Undercover,* Ted Nugent's *If You Can't Lick 'Em, Lick 'Em,* Accept's *Balls to the Wall,* and Exodus's *Pleasures of the Flesh.*

HOW EXPLICIT CAN YOU GET?

But the titles and covers are only the tip of the iceberg. It is the lyrics that make the sex-is-everything message so clear. Motley Crue's "Looks That Kill" refers to a young girl's genitalia as a "motor" she keeps clean, even though she's "a number thirteen." In his song, "Little Miss Dangerous," Ted Nugent described a young lady who is on fire for sex and "burns all night long." ZZ Top, in their album *Eliminator,* sang about a lover's legs and her proficiency in knowing "how to use them."

Formerly innocent-imaged Olivia Newton-John released the song "Culture Shock," which *People* magazine described as "a musical tribute to a ménage á trois."[1] Another tune, "Overnight Observation," is about a doctor seducing a woman patient.

If such explicit sexual descriptions shock you, hang on! Wait until you decipher the code language by which erotic lyrical images are conveyed. Automotive terms like "engine," "motor," and "machine" are all employed as sexual euphemisms. Teenagers who understand such language are cynically amused because Mom and Dad's moral objections to rock's lyrics have been cleverly circumvented. No wonder the music industry refers to sex-oriented tunes as "masturbatory rock."

"Where lyrics once used innuendoes, they are now overt. Where lyrics were once artfully suggestive, they are now blatantly explicit. Where lyrics once extolled tenderness and love in relationships, they now glorify violence and loveless sex. Have we forgotten the airwaves belong to the people?"—George David Weiss, president of the Song Writers Guild[2]

Some rock composers have included the subject of sadomasochism, inflicting physical pain for sexual pleasure. The Rolling Stones' "Beast of Burden" and John Cougar Mellencamp's "Hurt So Good" are examples of excursions into formerly forbidden territory.

Vinnie Vincent, former guitarist for KISS, commented on their songs "Shoot You Full of Love" and "I Want to Be Your Victim." He admitted, "The stuff in the album should be X-rated. It's really pornographic. A song like 'I Want to Be Your Victim' is the ultimate rock 'n' roll bondage number."[3]

The performers themselves almost arrogantly proclaim that they are selling sex. David Coverdale of the group Whitesnake says that their album titles like *Slide It In* and *Love Hunter* are about sex. Coverdale says, "Isn't sex what rock 'n' roll is all about?"[4] Nikki Sixx of Motley Crue says, "We're intellectuals on a crotch level."

The rock video phenomenon has made a star's appearance even more significant than before, for youth can watch such blatantly sexual performers as David Lee Roth in their own living rooms. He and such erotic performers as Billy Idol and Madonna can now be not only heard, but watched, twenty-four hours a day.

Who's to blame for such irresponsible exploitation? Who produces and promotes such warped ideas to pollute young minds? Certainly not teenagers themselves. Mercenary adults run the major record companies. Driven by greed, they care nothing about your child's morals and will descend to any depth to arouse teenage sexual curiosity.

IS GAY OK?

Unless you've been living in Outer Mongolia, you know only too well that today's child is faced with unprecedented homosexual influences. Keeping your child straight is no longer an assured outcome of child-rearing.

I have yet to meet the most liberal parent who wanted his child to become a homosexual. The gay life-style is an ongoing exercise in frustration, emotional ruin, and, with the coming of AIDS, a downright threat to life. With homosexuals coming out of the closet to assault society's morals, it was inevitable that rock music would deal with gay life-styles.

David Bowie is a well-known British singer/composer/guitarist who, in the past, boasted of his bisexuality in interviews and songs. He rose to fame over a decade ago, sporting orange hair and laced high-heeled boots, moving effeminately to a rock beat.

> "Rock music has become a plague of messages about sexual promiscuity, incest, sadomasochism, satanism, and misogyny. There is a connection between self-restraint and shame. An individual incapable of shame and embarrassment is probably incapable of the governance of the self. A public incapable of shame and embarrassment about public vulgarity is unsuited to self-government."—Columnist George Will *(Newsweek)*

Bowie portrayed acts of copulation on stage with other males while singing homosexual songs like "Queen Bitch."

On a sellout world tour in 1984, Boy George flaunted his bisexuality by announcing during the concerts that he would "like to sleep with each member of the audience individually." The cover of the album *Waking Up with the House on Fire* showed George with heavy makeup and a mane of luxurious red hair.

Elton John, pop music's talented pianist with the enormous glasses, has been fairly outspoken about his sexual deviations. He was involved for many years with his lyricist, Bernie Taupin.

The gay duo the Communards mixed leftist politics with disco rhythms, including on their 1988 album *Red* the song "There's More to Love Than Boy Meets Girl."

Youth can't help but notice that some rock

artists like Elton John and David Bowie appear to live rich, successful, and happy lives. Your child may know homosexuality is wrong, but how long can he fend off his rock idol's insistence that gay is good?

THE CONTROVERSY OVER PORN ROCK

Shocked though you may be, you probably must admit you know little of rock music and are unaware that sexually explicit albums are on public display throughout your city. Worse, they may be in your own home. Adult ignorance contributes to the proliferation of rock pornography marketed for your children. Consider what happened when, in 1985, some concerned parents and avaricious rock artists locked horns in Washington.

Susan Baker, wife of the Secretary of the Treasury James Baker, initiated the debate over porn rock after hearing her seven-year-old daughter listening to Madonna sing "Like a Virgin." The appalled Mrs. Baker stated, "The issue affects my family. I really believe that the escalation of violence and sexuality is a form of child abuse."[5] Tipper Gore, wife of Senator Albert Gore of Tennessee, expressed outrage at the lyrics of rock hits.

When the Senate Commerce Committee met, Mrs. Baker, Mrs. Gore, and others spoke on the issue. Senator Ernest Hollings of South Carolina declared, "The framers of the First Amendment never considered broadcast airwaves that would pipe this stuff willy-nilly into homes."[6]

There was a reaction in the rock camp, of course. Rocker Frank Zappa claimed the Washington wives behind the antiporn-rock campaign were "the wives of Big Brother." Zappa called the Washington wives "cultural terrorists" with "antisexual pseudo-Christian legislative fervor."[7]

But the Washington wives of the Parents Music Resource Center (PMRC) were not put off by such protests. After the Senate hearings they started stomping the media trail, warning America about the group Judas Priest advocating oral sex at gunpoint and Motley Crue describing quickie sex in an elevator. The PMRC pointed out that, between the seventh and twelfth grades, teens listen to an estimated ten thousand hours of rock music—the same amount of time they spend in twelve years of school.[8]

PMRC concerns were echoed by others. The National Education Association estimated that five thousand teenage suicides each year were linked to depression fueled by fatalistic lyrics.

The Washington wives and others who shared their concerns did win a victory of sorts. Twenty-two major record labels endorsed the proposal (made by the Recording Industry Association of America) that companies should print warning labels on albums or print lyrics if the songs contained explicit references to sex or violence.

While it remains to be seen how effective the push for music ratings will be, the PMRC has definitely had some effect. Blackie Lawless of the heavy metal group WASP complained that the group couldn't get bookings in many cities–including Las Vegas, of all places–because of the publicity generated by the PMRC. WASP claimed it planned to sue Tipper Gore.

This whole controversy has made it obvious that purveyors of porn like to appeal to the First Amendment. Knowing that most Americans prefer to think of themselves as free people in a free society, the producers and performers immediately began screaming "Hold on to your freedom!" as soon as concerned parents expressed their desire to warn buyers that the material is sexually explicit. They are not too interested, obviously, in protecting freedom in America unless *freedom* means the right to sell salacious material to impressionable youth.

CHAPTER

2

The Battle for Young Minds

TOO MUCH GETTING HIGH?

You may have done your best as a parent, but it's hard to counter that constant absorption of pro-drug, pro-alcohol attitudes prevalent in today's music. It's all there in the songs and lyrics and the public image of the rock stars whose records your child listens to.

Merely mentioning drugs in a song doesn't convey approval, but casual discussion of drug usage elevates the subject to a degree of familiarity and acceptance. Advertisers know that the desirability of a product to consumers is directly proportionate to the frequency of its mention. Drug users know this, too.

The Beatles sang, "I get high with a little help from my friends." The song became a pop standard, showing that our culture is desensitized to off-the-cuff drug references.

Cocaine is openly snorted at many recording studios. An arrest for drug violations is fashionable in some rock circles, certainly not rare. Consequently, if your child attends concerts and is later offered dope, he probably will view it as something his rock idol has used and

At a recent International Music Conference, the spokesman for a major record industry advertising firm stated: "Record companies and music publishers have earned many millions of dollars from extolling the virtues of drugs. Would one turn out phonograph records extolling the virtues of forceful rape, armed robbery, or kidnapping? The answer, I think, for many companies is yes, as long as there is money in it and they don't go to jail."

enjoyed. But your child's drug arrest won't be shrugged off as easily as that of wealthy rock stars represented by high-priced attorneys.

A list of prominent rock artists who have openly admitted drug usage would be too lengthy to recount. Some notable examples include Paul McCartney, Boy George, Jimmy Buffett, David Crosby, Stephen Stills, Joe Cocker, and Eric Clapton. Keith Richards of the Rolling Stones was charged with heroin possession. Mick Jagger of the Stones was presented with a silverplated snuff box for cocaine at a birthday party in Madison Square Garden.

Alcohol use among youth does not carry the dangers of being convicted for drug use, but it is increasing even more than drug use. Drinking does not have the mystique of drug use (since booze is legal, at least for adults), but alcohol is still the drug of choice for most

The Drug-Death Link in Rock

Jimi Hendrix ushered in the drug-death syndrome when he suffocated in a pool of his own vomit after an overdose. Within two weeks, Janis Joplin and Jim Morrison followed him to similar fates. Brian Jones of the Stones drowned while high in his swimming pool. Other victims include James Honeyman-Scott of the Pretenders, Tommy Bolin of Deep Purple, Sid Vicious of the Sex Pistols, Led Zeppelin drummer John Bonham, drummer Keith Moon of the Who, and AC/DC lead singer Bon Scott. Rock king Elvis Presley's body was like a human pincushion at the time of his death in 1977. The fact that most of the drugs involved in his death were prescribed made no difference. Both legal and illegal drugs can cause dependency and, in many instances, death.

youth. Rock artists are often notorious drinkers, as seen in this statement by Motley Crue member Nikki Sixx: "The only thing I care about is rock 'n' roll, chicks, and my bottle of Jack Daniels."[1] Some of the drug-related rock deaths mentioned above also involved alcohol.

Rock musicians, who use high-paid attorneys to beat their drug raps and spend thousands on operations and detoxification programs to patch up their bodies, owe their popularity to the patronage of young fans who have financed such high living.

EAST MEETS WEST: CULTS IN ROCK

Many parents are concerned about the Eastern religions and cults that have influenced and led astray many young people. Through repeated exposure to some recordings, the teenage mind of the West is meeting the religious philosophies of the East and becoming vulnerable to their attraction.

An early album by the Moody Blues, *In Search of the Lost Chord,* referred to the mystical concept of a musical chord with supernatural vibrations. If that exact chord can be struck, the listener is said to gain instant enlightenment through a transcendent state. Inside, the album sleeve pictured a yantra, the visual equivalent of the verbal chant known as the mantra. While the record is played, the listener is told to stare at the geometric designs and thereby enter an altered state of consciousness.

An album by the group Yes was entitled *Tales from Topographic Oceans.* The jacket explained that the lyrics were based on Hindu scriptures and were specifically inspired by Paramahansa Yogananda's book, *Autobiography of a Yogi.* The songs of the album were said to reveal "the science of God."

Former Beatle George Harrison's records are not only a tool of Eastern evangelism, but a significant portion of the proceeds from their sales goes to support the Hare Krishna cult.

Airport travelers have been accosted by cult members who solicit for donations in exchange for a copy of *Bhagavad-Gita as It Is*. Harrison wrote its foreword.

Why has George Harrison so zealously expounded Eastern mysticism? In his days with the Beatles, he turned John, Paul, and Ringo eastward to the Maharishi Mahesh Yogi. Harrison was a practicing Hindu as early as 1967, long before today's assorted gurus and Krishna Consciousness chanters gained popularity. Since the early days of the Maharishi, his faith in Hinduism has grown. Witness his composition "My Sweet Lord": The song is a prayer of dedication to Lord Krishna, an incarnation of the Hindu godhead and supposedly the central figure in the *Bhagavad-Gita*, probably the best-loved of Hindu sacred writings.

Rock music isn't the only conveyor of Eastern religious thought in our culture. Mysticism is heralded on television and in the press. Actress and author Shirley MacLaine is probably the best-known propagator of Eastern (and New Age) thought. Rock isn't the only offender, but, perhaps most dangerously, it's the one least suspected by parents.

SATANIC ROCKING

If your son walked in the house with *The Satanic Bible* under his arm, it would go straight to the trash can. But is the stereo in your child's room an altar to darkness that dispenses the devil's liturgy?

This may sound fanatical. After all, rock is

heard everywhere today. Could anything so pervasive be sinister? Be prepared for a jolt.

The list of entertainers who have ventured into the occult reads like a Who's Who of rock royalty. Elton John's lyricist, Bernie Taupin, once decorated his walls with satanic art and said, "The occult fascinates me." A German band went to the extreme of calling itself Lucifer's Friend and offered fans "devilishly good rock 'n' roll," calling one release "the demonic new album."

Foremost rock occultist Ritchie Blackmore of Deep Purple admits he has attended seances "to get closer to God" and sometimes leaves his body (astral projection) to float about the concert hall during performances.[2] He has recorded in a seventeenth-century castle supposedly haunted by a demon, who is a servant of the Babylonian god Baal.[3]

Formerly the lead guitarist for Led Zeppelin, Jimmy Page runs a close second to Blackmore in occult inclinations. Page once owned an occult bookstore and revered the late, infamous British spiritualist, Aleister Crowley. Noted for murders and sexual perversion, Crowley was so evil he renamed himself "The Beast 666."[4]

Fleetwood Mac also flirted with the occult. Their hit "Rhiannon" was about a Welsh witch. Singer Stevie Nicks has dedicated songs during concerts to "all the witches of the world."

Few groups could top the Rolling Stones for displays of blatant interest in evil. One of their early albums was entitled *Their Satanic Majesties Request*. For the cover, they posed as witches. A Richards-Jagger composition, "Sympathy for the Devil," became an unofficial satanic anthem.

The ultimate Stones embodiment of dark images came on their album *Goat's Head Soup,* part of which was recorded at a Haitian voodoo ritual. Behind the music are heard screams from those who are becoming possessed of evil spirits. One song, "Dancing with Mr. D.," describes a graveyard romp with the devil. A color picture inside the album shows a severed goat's head floating in a boiling cauldron. The goat's head is the universal symbol of Satan worship.

HEAVY METAL MADNESS

Heavy metal isn't a new element on a physics periodic chart, nor is it an industrial product conceived for the construction industry. Heavy metal is a kind of rock music spawned in the late sixties and alive and well in the eighties.

Those who listen to heavy metal are called "head bangers," alluding to the musical energy and excitement that makes fans bang their heads on the foot of the concert stage. The term "heavy metal" came from a description of its sound, comparing the crashing guitar chords to a Detroit assembly line.

Rock critic Lester Bangs defines it specifically: "In its classic form, it features plodding, unsubtle rhythms, screaming vocals, primal wailing guitar sounds, and macho-posturing lyrics dealing with sex, drugs, and rock 'n' roll."

A more analytical description was featured

Confronting Satanic Rock

Suppose you discover your child listens to satanic music. Perhaps he owns such records. As a concerned parent, you want to take action. What can you do?

Pose the following questions to him:

1. Does purchasing a record enhance the artist's popularity and more widely disperse his philosophy?

When a rock artist is idolized by millions of impressionable youth, his outlook on the demonic may be more inviting because of his commercial success. Certainly, no moral young person would want his peers to experiment with the occult simply because his favorite rock star recommends it.

2. If music has the ability to convey spiritual power as well as melodic and

in *Rolling Stone* magazine, which declared, "Heavy metal may not be high art, but it is heroic and its heroes assume one of several poses: sexual athletes (AC/DC); the ascendency to manhood via a variant on knife-wielding juvenile delinquency (Twisted Sister); insane instrumental virtuosity (Yngwie Malmsteen); the good old transcendent rock 'n' roll party ethic (Scorpions and Ratt); or any combination thereof (Motley Crue)."[5]

rhythmic content, what is implied when a musician admits contact with the power of darkness?

Pagan rituals conjure demons by rhythmic repetition and idolatrous devotion. Beware, then, of musical performers who misuse creativity to invest occult power in their art.

3. Is it possible to listen to the music of a rock artist involved in the occult and appreciate his talent without being affected by his lyrics or demonic inspiration?

Satan can use music to create an unhealthy spiritual atmosphere. The subconscious mind, the seat of the soul, is affected.

All occult phenomena comes from Satan, the enemy of God. Therefore, anyone who advocates demonic practices declares himself in opposition to the Lord. The devil relentlessly pursues your child's sympathy, so pray that he makes the right decision.

Heavy metal is popular. *Billboard,* the music industry's trade publication, commented, "Heavy metal has proved immune to shifting musical/cultural trends. Since 1980, no other pop music form has accounted for greater record sales. Of the top-grossing live acts in 1985, 20.6 percent were metal artists."[6]

Heavy metal is more than music. It's an image conjured by the artist's actions and stage antics. Heavy metal fashion features leather

Popular Heavy Metal Acts

- AC/DC
- Aerosmith
- Anthrax
- Blue Oyster Cult
- Bon Jovi
- Boston
- Cinderella
- Def Leppard
- Dio
- Dokken
- Europe
- Guns 'n' Roses
- Grateful Dead
- Iron Maiden
- Judas Priest
- KISS
- Yngwie Malmsteen
- Megadeth
- Metallica
- Motley Crue
- Motorhead
- Ozzy Osbourne
- Poison
- Queensryche
- Quiet Riot
- Ratt
- David Lee Roth
- Scorpions
- Slayer
- Twisted Sister
- Van Halen
- Venom
- Vinnie Vincent Invasion
- WASP
- White Lion
- Whitesnake

> "The essential element of heavy metal is the same as it was in the original 1950s rock 'n' roll: Parents hate it."—Twisted Sister's lead singer, Dee Snyder

costumes adorned with spikes, studs, and chains.

A label called Metal Blade Records, whose symbol is an axe blade dripping with blood, has released an album called *Metal Massacre Seven* with the symbol of death holding a scythe in one hand and a leashed Doberman pinscher in the other. An album by Hyrax is called *Raging Violence*. The jacket shows a head full of bullet holes, the skull splintering and the face grimacing in pain.

Rockie Shayes of the group Wrathchild wears the usual heavy metal regalia of leather and studs and has dozens of sharp three-inch spikes sticking out of his costume. Their stage show features naked women, whips, and chains. Shayes says, "I admit we're loud, lewd, and a little more than crazy, but what's wrong with it? If our wicked minds can think of something depraved, there's no doubt we'll put it to music and record it."[7]

The group Lizzy Borden features a macabre stage show. Their theatrical bloodletting is based on the band's namesake, the nineteenth-century murderer, Lizzy Borden, who killed her parents with an ax. The lead vocalist for the group says, "Although we like beheadings and killings—that's the stuff we grew up on watching TV—we're a product of our environment."[8]

Heavy metal audiences are young. A survey of those attending heavy metal concerts showed that 56 percent of the crowd was seventeen years of age or younger. Two-thirds were male. Only 9 percent of the heavy metal audience was twenty-four or older.[9] Such facts disturb California psychologist, Dr. Richard Sherman. He says, "Some of these groups project an image that can trigger violence, even blood and devil worship. When children choose them as role models, they're learning to go against the basic values of society."[10]

More sexy than satanic, the band Cinderella is an example of rock 'n' roll sexism at its worst. Their tune "Shake Me" describes a one-night stand with repeated acts of intercourse. Sex is a prominent element in most heavy metal acts, as shown in a 1988 concert by the group Guns 'n' Roses: fans tossed condoms on the stage during the performance.

"I WANT MY MTV!"

A vid-blitz has shaken Hollywood and the record business, establishing a whole new way of relating to music.

MTV—Music Television—is a cable TV channel that offers round-the-clock music videos. Launched in August 1981, MTV now boasts 13.5 million viewers, mostly between the ages of twelve and thirty-four. An average

De-Metalling Youth

An organization called Back in Control Center urges parents to "de-metal" kids who go off the deep end. The center says parents should take away heavy metal records, paraphernalia, and monitor clothes and friendships. Darlene Pettinicchio calls herself the center's "heavy metal consultant." She says, "We're talking about kids who become totally absorbed in punk or heavy metal, who dress like their favorite band, who act like band members, who get their philosophies and beliefs from band members."[11]

viewer spends sixty-eight minutes a day watching MTV (ninety minutes on Saturdays and Sundays).[12] Sixty-three percent of the audience is under age twenty-five.[13] Considered a risky oddity when it was launched, the twenty-four-hour music video channel has become a fixture in American life.

Music videos create a strange fantasy world where the bizarre is normal and few coherent story lines exist. The videos are mostly blatant visual gluttony, often saturated with sex, violence, and quick camera cuts that bombard the senses. Videos combine the power of rock music with thirty years of television technology and the razzle-dazzle of short, high-budget commercials. This is television that is seductive and addictive, especially to preteens.

The images are often repulsive. In one video

a nude woman in chains appears in the background while a man in the foreground sharpens a razor. In another, wild-haired, scantily clad vixens crawl on the outside of a steel cage, craving the bodies inside. Enslaved women appear in bondage with scenes of nudity and fondling. Most teens would recognize these scenes from videos of Billy Idol's "Dancing with Myself," the Scorpions' "Rock You Like a Hurricane," and Van Halen's "Oh, Pretty Woman."[14]

Sexy singer David Lee Roth carried his sensuous stage act into living rooms with his "Yankee Rose" video. Simulating copulation, Roth gave viewers three minutes of overt sensuality that had no parallel in previous videos. The camera apparently had a fixation on the crotches and behinds of Roth and his band.

Madonna's video for "Like a Virgin" shows her writhing on a bed in a wedding gown, dancing half-clothed on a gondola, and wearing a white underwire corset. In the video for "Open Your Heart to Me" she is working in a peep show and, at the video's end, scampering off down the road with a young boy, suggesting that she is going to initiate him sexually.

This is typical of rock videos. Woman are often pictured as nymphomaniacs wearing spiked heels and black lingerie, parading through the rock 'n' roll jungle anticipating seduction. Sadomasochism often enters into the sexual experience, promoting rapist fantasies that lurk in the recesses of the American male's mind.

MTV did ban the 1988 Motley Crue video for

> "Seeing a sexy video can teach you that if you're not sexually active, there's something wrong with you. Once you've depicted the song, you've magnified the effect a hundredfold."—Dr. Victor Strasburger, Director of Adolescent Medicine for the American Academy of Pediatrics Task Force on Television[15]

"You're All I Need," which an MTV spokesman described as "excessively violent." MTV also banned Billy Idol's "Hot in the City," which showed his girlfriend hanging on a plexiglas crucifix. But such bans are almost unknown.

Sex isn't the only thing that needs censoring. Violence has been part of rock videos since the beginning. The National Coalition on Television Violence (NCTV) studied nine hundred rock videos and reported that 46 percent contained violence or indicated violence. Of the nine hundred, 13 percent had sadistic violence with an attacker deriving pleasure from his violent act.

With young children watching these scenes of women in chains and people being tortured and shot, psychologist Joyce Brothers is worried. "Teenagers have not fused the idea of love and sex. So when you teach them that violence and sex are related, it's extremely dangerous for their future behavior."[16]

Even people in the rock music industry have expressed concern. One disc jockey says, "The scary element is that kids are at the most

Coping with Videos

Parents can do the obvious thing with MTV—turn it off. It is odd that parents often complain about television's effects on youth but seldom eliminate it. Perhaps a less drastic alternative would be to learn to watch it with a critical eye and to discuss it with youth. In the words of *Newsweek,* "Parental supervision may be the sanest answer to any threat posed by music video."[17] Parents can take the time to sit and watch it with youth and then discuss the images. Better, they can find recreation that is more interesting than passively watching the tube. Most sensitive parents would agree with Peggy Charren of Action for Children's Television, who said, "If there are enough alternatives in a child's life, you don't have to worry about what they see on TV."[18]

impressionable point of their lives, and I would not want any of my sons to get their attitudes about sex and violence or women from music videos."[19]

In all fairness to the artists and the producers of videos, many rock videos show genuine creativity. A-ha's "Take on Me," Men at Work's "Who Can It Be Now?" Queen's "A Kind of Magic," Phil Collins's "Land of Confusion," and Madness' "Our House" showed that performers could do more than generate bizarre, unsettling images. Many Christian rock artists—Amy Grant, DeGarmo and Key, and many others—now produce quality videos. These are a welcome alternative to many of the secular products.

CHAPTER

3

Who's Who in Rock

Just when a parent thinks he vaguely understands the rock scene, teenagers employ their favorite tactic: "Why can't I listen to such-and-such rock group? They aren't homosexuals, they don't use drugs, and they don't sing about sex. Can I buy one of their albums?"

The following glossary of rock music performers was compiled with this dilemma in mind. It would be impossible to include every performer on the charts. Some of the better-known groups with the highest record sales in recent years have been listed.

What if your children bring up a name not included here? (They will.) The group or person may have gained public attention after this book's publication. New bands form, old bands break up, performers die, and other changes occur. You can't keep up with all of it, but at least try to be aware of who is and is not recording.

There is no hard-and-fast definition for *rock star.* Iron Maiden is definitely a rock act, but what about Genesis, Olivia Newton-John, and Paul Simon? Such performers as these are usually considered *pop* artists, and they are not dealt with in this glossary.

Pop performers often have immoral lifestyles and sing questionable lyrics, but most don't exhibit that sex-obsessed, anti-establishment attitude of so many rock performers.

My analyses may seem slanted toward the unsavory aspects of rock artists, neglecting positive elements in their character and music. But what is positive isn't problematic. For this reason, some popular artists such as Phil Collins, Michael Jackson, Bruce Springsteen, Lionel Ritchie, and others are not included because, for the most part, their lyrics and lifestyles are not openly immoral.

AC/DC

In the 1980s, five delinquents from Down Under imported to America the firebrand hard rock that had captivated Aussies. The source of their name is controversial. According to the rock periodical *Circus*, AC/DC connotes "power and sexual ambiguity."[1]

Dirty Deeds Done Dirt Cheap, their re-released 1978 album, said it all. Their "deeds" delineated lyrics and graphics too explicit to print here. AC/DC song titles include "Big Balls," "Love at First Feel," "Let Me Put My Love into You," and "Highway to Hell." The latter was delivered with a lascivious growl by lead singer, Bon Scott. Overtly inviting Satan to claim his soul, Scott declared hell to be the "promised land" and warned that nothing would stop him from cashing in his "season ticket" for a "one-way ride." Later, Scott, aged thirty-three, died from an alcohol/drug overdose. One prorock journal commented on Scott's death by observing, "Throughout the AC/DC catalogue there is a disturbing correlation between pleasure/sex/drunkenness and unconsciousness/death, which has now reached its tragic culmination."[2]

The group found a new singer in Brian Johnson, and hit the road again declaring in their new album that they were *Back in Black*. "Hells Bells," a hit off of the new album, showed no signs of sobered repentance. "If you're into evil," Johnson sang, "you are most certainly a friend of mine." The 1988 album *Blow Up Your Videos* also made it clear that the band had undergone no change in attitude.

Commenting on the band's nasty image, vocalist Brian Johnson stated, "A number of moms and dads were very upset about having their kids called 'devil worshipers,' but we knew everything would turn full circle, and thanks to Jim and Tammy Bakker, it has. Who's the real sinner now?"[3]

AEROSMITH

The soft sounds of the 1970s didn't deter this hard-driving Boston band. Their albums sold millions, and one of them, *Toys in the Attic*, was on the charts for 150 weeks. Audiences of 80,000 came to hear them churn out deadening metal sounds and profane lyrics.

The group focused on its androgynous lead

singer, Steve Tyler. Tyler crooned of the cheerleader who was a "young bleeder" and the short-skirted girl with a "kitty in the middle." When police busted fifty-two young people for drug abuse at one of its concerts, Aerosmith paid $3,650 to bail them out. Tyler boasted of his arrest for drugs while in the eleventh grade.

When Aerosmith regrouped after several years' absence from the rock scene, its ardor for evil hadn't subsided. Joe Perry declared, "Everybody does drugs. Everyone has their own drugs, whether it's eating [sexual expletive] or being gay. I'm not advocating them and I don't choose to do them before I go on stage, but when you go on the road there's nothing to do but to do drugs and [sexual expletive]."

The band's "reunion" album was *Done with Mirrors,* which did little to prove that the band had mellowed. *Billboard* magazine commented of their new act, "Elaborate staging was eschewed in favor of antic behavior and liberal use of obscenities . . . and the one word of more than four letters Steve Tyler uttered begins with 'mother.' "[4] The 1987 album *Permanent Vacation* confirmed that Aerosmith was "business as usual." However, band member Tom Hamilton stated in a recent interview, "We can see clearly now, unlike all those years of playing under that haze of pot, booze, and whatever else."[5]

BLACK SABBATH

Former lead singer Ozzy Osbourne has his own idea about how this British group got the name. He says, "We were sitting around, and this old Boris Karloff horror movie came on television. It was called 'Black Sabbath.' Everybody was talking around preaching peace and love, but we wanted to go in the opposite direction. We formed Black Sabbath to explore the darker side of everyone's personality."[6]

Their career began with publicity stunts like holding black masses before concerts (complete with a nude on an altar sprinkled with chicken blood). Their first album pictured the inverted cross of Christ. A later album, *Sabbath, Bloody Sabbath,* depicted a nude satanic ritual with the numbers 666 emblazoned across the front, associations that made the name Black Sabbath seem appropriate. Their aggressiveness, the droning lyrics, and blast-furnace bass fit their public relations image.

An album entitled *Born Again* featured a demonic baby with satanic horns, fangs, and claws on its fingers. Lyrics spoke of a "prince of evil" that fought for people's minds. An ad in *Billboard* magazine for *Born Again* featured a hexagram with black magic symbols and the byline, "Hitting below the Bible Belt."

Their album *Mob Rules,* released in late 1981, showed hooded beings with no faces holding whips in their hands. A sheet hangs in the center with the horned visage of Lucifer etched in blood.

The band has gone through several changes since lead singer Ozzy's departure. For awhile, Ian Gillan, formerly with Deep Purple, took over the job. When asked about the satanic aspects of the band, Gillan said, "I don't know if Tony and Geezer [band members] were into devil worship or not. All I know is that when we were recording the album *Born Again,* which we did at this big castle, they would wake up at four in the afternoon. I don't know what they would do. They wouldn't start recording until late at night."[7]

Tony Iommi, lead singer, commented on Black Sabbath's evil aspects by declaring, "Various things of the world beyond I've always had a deep fascination for. That's the supernatural, an area I'm very interested in."[8] Interestingly, the group's 1988 album was titled *The Eternal Idol.*

BON JOVI

The band is composed of Tico Torres on drums, Richie Sambora on guitar, David Bryan on keyboards, and Alic John-Such on bass. But it's Bon Jovi, guitar in hand and long curls flying, who attracts attention. His parents encouraged an early interest in music by giving him an acoustic guitar. The first commercial success came when the album *7800 Fahrenheit* sold more than five hundred thousand copies. Later came the double-platinum album *Slippery When Wet,* which made real stars of Bon Jovi.

Recorded in Vancouver, the album credits the city with being the stripper capital of the world and inspiring the album title. Bon Jovi described one night in a stripper bar when an unclad young woman showering in a Plexiglas booth tried to get his attention by rubbing against the booth.[9] Consequently, the original cover for the album showed a dancer in a wet T-shirt. When radio stations and distributors complained, the cover was changed to a rain-slicked black surface with the title finger-scrawled across it. But the inner sleeve still had pictures of scantily clad girls washing cars.

Bon Jovi's first hit single was "You Give Love a Bad Name." According to the lyrics, the girl with the angel smile puts the man through hell. "The damage is done . . . you're to blame . . . you give love a bad name." With their libidinous attitude, Bon Jovi gives caring love a very bad name.

BOSTON

For hard-rockers who lamented the popularity of disco and softer sounds, Boston was a welcome, deafening sonic relief. Led by Tom Scholz, a twenty-nine-year-old MIT graduate, Boston's first album soared from obscurity to sell 3.5 million copies. (Scholz worked in the Research and Development Division of Polaroid and has been described as an electronic genius.) Riding to success on its initial hit, "More Than a Feeling," Boston triggered enthusiastic audience response by asking for marijuana joints as a prelude to their tune "Smokin'." After an extended absence from the music scene, they returned in the mid-eighties much mellower, as their hit "Amanda" testified.

DAVID BOWIE

Newsweek called British star Bowie "the single most influential rock artist of the last ten years." The first pop music star to openly proclaim his homosexuality, David Bowie set the stage for other artists to come out of the closet. Bowie also confessed to drug addiction, from heroin to cocaine. He admits, "Actually, I was junked out of my mind most of the time. You can do good things with drugs, but then comes the long decline."[10] Bowie said of the medium that propelled his rise to stardom, "Rock 'n' roll has always been the devil's music. It could well bring about a very evil feeling in the West."[11]

References to decadence in his songs and performances are too numerous to mention. Perhaps his own flaunting of perversion is what led Bowie to finally conclude, "I've never been in love. Love is a disease that breeds jealousy, anxiety, and brute anger."[12]

When his ex-wife, Angela Bowie, was asked how it felt to be married to "the world's king faggot," she replied, "I think it's great. It all depends upon your knowledge of gay culture, of which I can happily say I'm a member." *Time* reported, "Thursday night was gay night. David would go to a gay club, Angie to a lesbian club, and they would bring home people they found."

Older and wiser, Bowie now condemns the drug-oriented, morally loose environment of the rock culture. He refers to it as an influence that "hasn't done anything except produce casualties."[13]

BOY GEORGE

More than a decade after David Bowie introduced drag into rock, Boy George flounced upon the scene in fancy prints and pancake makeup, declaring, "I don't believe people should be defined by their sexuality. I don't believe in male or female. I'm not particularly masculine, and I'm not particularly feminine. I don't think it matters."[14]

Going against the grain of most lead rock singers, who typically strike a macho pose, Boy George was deliberately sexless, sporting a porkpie hat and shapeless smocks. (In the early eighties both Michael Jackson and Boy George seemed almost innocent in their lack of masculinity.) Fans mimicked his braided hair and smocks. And they were enchanted by his group Culture Club's curious mixture of soul and white rhythm and blues.

But Boy George wasn't as innocent as he appeared. Some of the songs' lyrics smacked of homosexuality, with tunes like "I'll Tumble 4 Ya," suggesting homosexual oral sex. While such songs were selling like crazy, his affair with another member of the group became well-known.

His spiritual views were described bluntly in another interview: "I don't believe in God, that there's somebody up there with a bowl of rice waiting to feed us. I believe in life after death. I think we all end up as maggots and that sort of thing. After all, we fertilize the earth."[15]

When Culture Club accepted a Grammy Award as the best new artist of 1983, George puckishly praised the American television audience for recognizing "a good drag queen when you see one."[16]

In 1986, Boy George came out of another closet—the drug closet. He was arrested and charged with heroin possession. The parents of a young man who died of a drug overdose in his apartment filed a multimillion dollar suit. Boy George had once said, "I don't do drugs. I never have."[17]

ALICE COOPER

Vincent Furnier, a preacher's son from Arizona, rose to fame as Alice Cooper by giving his fans exhibitions of transvestitism, snakes, mutilated chickens, and mock public executions. His albums explored ever-deepening stages of perversion. *School's Out* featured its vinyl encased in disposable women's panties. *Billion Dollar Babies* pictured a baby made up with Cooper-style mascara. *Muscle of Love* extolled the pleasure of masturbation. *Welcome to My Nightmare* was staged by Alice simulating necrophiliac sex with a lifelike mannequin. *Alice Cooper Goes to Hell* brought the rouge-rock queen to an encounter with the devil, referred to as "the greatest, number one."

For a while it seemed Alice's age and physical exhaustion had caught up with him. Attempting a return to fame, Cooper recorded an album entitled *Constrictor.* On the front of the record, a live boa constrictor entwines itself around his face and neck, and part of the snake's body disappears into his mouth. For his promotional tour, Alice featured the usual doll decapitations and bloodbaths on stage. He added two scantily clad females, whom he attacked with whips.[18]

Though older and (supposedly) dried out, Alice Cooper has no intention of changing his style. His 1987 album *Raise Your Fist and Yell* featured the usual grotesque cover and psychotic lyrics. In an interview on his 1987 tour he stated, "I want to take everyone on an emotional roller coaster. I want them to feel the madness."[19]

DEF LEPPARD

Entitled *Pyromania*, the album jacket featured a burning skyscraper with a gun sight centered over the most intense portion of the flame. If you think an album portraying arson isn't humorous, neither are Def Leppard's other antics. Their tune "Photograph," a song about sexual frustration, speaks of caged women flashing switchblades. Joe Elliot of the band says, "People always ask me how we got the name of Def Leppard. Actually, it came from a poster depicting a rather strange-looking jungle cat with a hearing horn in his ear."[20] None of the members claim to use drugs, but Elliot says, "We used to drink a lot. Now we drink more."[21]

Billboard magazine said of the British group's fans, "They are the classic example of stand-on-the-chairs, wave-your-fist, scream-yourself-hoarse audience. They call this headbanger music, not so much for its sheer volume but because it's about as subtle as being hit between the eyes with a two-by-four."[22] Sexual images are also included in their music, such as "Rock-Rock ('Til You Drop)" declaring, "Come along with me, your mama don't mind what your mama don't see."

But most disturbing is their so-called arson-oriented rock and the irresponsibility of choosing such reprehensible themes. What can be expected when Joe Elliot says, "When we recorded this album, we tried to get ourselves as drunk as possible."[23] To no one's surprise, the 1987 album was titled *Hysteria*.

DIO (RONNIE JAMES DIO)

His album *Holy Diver* pictures a cleric wrapped in chains being thrust into the sea. Standing above him as tormentor is a symbol of Satan, a horned figure with his index and little fingers extended in the satanic salute. Dressing in black and admitting to astral-projecting on stage, Dio has been accused of satanic collusion. Dio says, "Just because I choose to explore topics that touch on mythology, I'm labeled a devil worshiper. At least I understand something about the occult, which is more than I can say about certain bands that use pentagrams and upside-down crosses as their emblems."

But Dio's lyrics aren't as convincing as his protestation. In the song "The Last in Line," he talks about going off to see a witch, declaring, "We may never come home." He then says we are all born "upon the cross" to learn if we are "evil or divine." The stage for his "Sacred

Heart" album tour featured a leering, red-eyed creature symbolizing Satan. Dio declares, "There's so many negative things associated with heavy metal these days – blood, guts, and a mentality that often seems nonexistent – our music is escape from reality."[24]

Adding to the ambivalence, Dio says, "Jimmy Page [former lead guitarist for Led Zeppelin] is heavily into black magic. I've just been involved in white magic, which is for good and not for bad, by that I mean like having contact with the spirit world via seances."[25] An interesting statement, considering that his 1987 album was titled *Dream Evil*.

EURYTHMICS

What Boy George did for male androgyny, Annie Lennox of the Eurythmics duo did for female gender-benders. Throughout her early career she emphasized sexual ambiguity. At a Grammy Awards show she performed dressed as Elvis Presley, complete with sideburns. The video for "Who's That Girl?" ended with Annie as both a man and a woman, kissing herself. Annie stated, "I never felt cross-dressing took away my femininity." Later Annie adopted a new image, seen in sexy publicity shots in which she wore a black lace bra. Her once orange hair was dyed platinum.

This British duo – Annie Lennox and Dave Stewart – exemplifies the slick, synthesized pop-rock sound that appeals to both teens and adults. Annie and Dave have produced such repetitive but interesting hits as "Sweet Dreams Are Made of This," "Here Comes the Rain Again," and "Love Is a Stranger." Annie, a former model, has a beautiful face, but her shortly cropped hair (almost a crewcut), men's ties, and stage manner exude a sadomasochistic air. This became obvious in the video for "Thorn in My Side," showing leather-clad women giving the brush-off to men. "Sweet Dreams Are Made of This" also suggests sadomasochism: "Some of them want to abuse you, some of them want to be abused." The song "Sisters Are Doing It for Themselves" was a hymn to women doing without men. One wonders what effect such macho-mannered women as Annie have on the femininity of female fans.

FOREIGNER

The touching "I Want to Know What Love Is" was a Number 1 hit for this group, but it is not typical of their work. The 1985 song about the search for true love differs radically from their other hits: "Dirty White Boy," "Waiting for a Girl Like You," and "Cold as Ice." "Hot-blooded," a major hit in 1978, asked a young girl the question, "Come on, baby, can you do more than dance?" and tried to coax her away for a quick sexual encounter. "Urgent" is self-explanatory; it is an expression of desire for a brief sexual fling, with no commitment or desire for love. Listeners who enjoyed "I Want to Know What Love Is" need to know that

Foreigner, like so many rock bands, sings more about salacious sex than about genuine love.

THE GRATEFUL DEAD

This San Francisco band began in the flower power era but is still going strong. Perennial promoters of acid rock, they stage shows for their devoted fans, "Dead-heads," whose attendance is marked by drug usage. Lead guitarist Jerry Garcia has been convicted for possession of cocaine, pot, and LSD. Keyboard player Ron "Pigpen" McKernan, considered the band's most creative musician, died from the ingestion of alcohol and drugs. The message seems lost on those remaining. Jerry Garcia stated, "Our lives are controlled by music,"[26] but the role of drugs seems as important as music for this band, a leftover from the counterculture movement of the 1960s.

BILLY IDOL

His real name is William Broad. He was originally a punk rocker with the group Generation X. He assumed the name Billy Idol because he believed, "I can be an idol just by calling myself one." His combination of hostile rebel and sexual athlete repels adults but entrances kids. In the video for his song "White Wedding" he jams a ring on the bride's finger, causing it to bleed. In "Dancing with Myself" he shows a woman hanging in chains. The song "Rebel Yell" speaks of his lover at midnight crying, "More, more, more." "Flesh for Fantasy" describes making love "navel to navel" with a woman who can "see and feel my sex attack."

"Rebellion and sexuality are the real bookends of rock 'n' roll. I'm glad there's someone around like me who says what he thinks," Idol declares.[27] Part of his appeal is his sexually threatening image – black leather pants (which he often removes), tattered T-shirts (which he always removes), spiked wristbands, and a perpetual sneer. When he performs, he constantly strokes his body and writhes sensuously. Of drugs he says, "Drugs don't really alter your perception or anything that much. I mean they do, but I think if you are pretty much in control of who you are, then drugs aren't really a problem."[28]

IRON MAIDEN

In the days of Elvis and Fats Domino, who would have dreamed that a group would record an album of praise to the Antichrist? *The Number of the Beast* was such an album, and it featured such lines as "the number of the Beast, the one for you and me." The official mascot for Iron Maiden is Eddie, a metal skeleton symbolizing death. Eddie was pictured on the cover of *The Number of the Beast*, along with Satan, luring souls into hell. Seven of the eight songs on the album pertain to death and assorted evils. The one exception is "22 Acacia Avenue," a song about a prostitute.

When Steve Harris, bassist for the band, was confronted about charges of Satanism, he admitted that during recording of the album there were mysterious power failures, instances of amps blowing up, and radio interference.

Ex-drummer Clive Burr said, "We really don't believe in black magic. We're just interested in it."[29] Bruce Dickinson of the band says, "We're about as anti-Satan as a band can get."[30] But the touring stage for their album *Power Slave* featured a pyramid with the eye of the Egyptian god, Horus. Dickinson admits the song "Peace of Mind" refers to Tarot card symbols. He also admits that much of what he writes and sings is based on mythology and Egyptian black magic.

The 1985 album *Live After Death* pictures their skeletal mascot Eddie rising out of the grave. The futuristic album *Somewhere in Time* features Eddie as a bionic death symbol, marching down the streets of a *Blade Runner* city, ray gun in hand.

The words to "Heaven Can Wait" are of little comfort to those who are hoping the band's satanic imagery is only a joke. The singer speaks of the "angel of death," who's coming after his soul. The song declares, "Heaven can wait, I have a lust for the earth below." Speaking of such songs, Steve Harris says, "I'm not sure what I believe, although I do believe there are things out there that are unexplainable. The more mysterious a topic is, whether it's the occult or science fiction, the more fun it is to write about."[31]

ELTON JOHN

The piano's current popularity as a rock instrument reflects the influence and talent of British star Elton John. Noted for his musical genius and clever melodies, John has sung of topics as diverse as lesbianism ("All the Young Girls Love Alice") and glue sniffing ("The Bitch Is Back"). (Thankfully, most of his songs are much less controversial. "Your Song" and "Good-bye, Yellow Brick Road" are examples of the best in rock.)

His success has helped him buy himself two hundred pairs of eyeglasses worth $40,000. In 1987 and 1988 he toured the world, playing the piano while wearing an *Amadeus*-style coat and powdered wig.

John's musical talent commands respect, but his moral views are highly questionable. He has admitted being both suicidal and bisexual. He told *Rolling Stone*, "There's nothing wrong with going to bed with somebody of your own sex. I just think people should be very free with sex—they should draw the line at goats."[32]

In February 1984 he married a sound engineer. (The marriage eventually failed.) His wife declared, "I've heard all sorts of stories about Elton and that he's supposed to be bisexual, but that doesn't worry me."[33] The press described Bob Halley, John's personal assistant and live-in lover for many years, as "mute with shock." For many years prior, John was involved with his brilliant lyricist, Bernie Taupin. Regarding his homosexuality, John told a rock periodical, "I think it hurt my record sales because it's not everybody's cup of tea. I just had to get it off my chest. I expected to offend quite a few people, but I'd rather be honest than to live my life as lie. I don't flaunt it, but I thought I could help other people like that."[34]

JUDAS PRIEST

With stage props ranging from smoke bombs to bullwhips, the bellicose, leather-clad heavy metal group Judas Priest looks like it sounds. Appropriately, violence accompanies this British group wherever it goes. During a 1984 concert, fans caused considerable damage to Madison Square Garden. The band's Rob Halford declared, "I like to think of what we do as controlled decadence. We want to stress the violence and volume, but we don't want that to be viewed as a negative element. Rock 'n' roll is the last safe outlet for hostility and tension."[35] Album titles like *Screaming for Vengeance, Killing Machine,* and *Hell Bent for Leather* express the hostility.

Glen Tipton of the group says, "In actual fact, our image off stage isn't too dissimilar from our image on stage. We don't dress drastically different. We don't live in two different worlds."[36] Halford states, "Sure, there may be a few unsavory things in our music, a bit of tension and hostility, but that's what the world is about these days."[37]

If there is hostility in the music, there is also sex. In one photograph, Rob Halford appears on a motorcycle with a scantily clad girl in leather riding behind him. She wears a studded collar with an attached chain that Halford holds in his hand. When asked if he was personally involved in the sadomasochistic love-torture techniques parodied in performances, Halford replied, "To a certain extent. Sexually, I have always been to the fullest extent of the experience that S & M has to offer. It's nice to experiment by yourself and get off on whatever you get off on."[38] If that isn't enough, the tune "Eat Me Alive" describes oral sex so vividly the lyrics are unprintable.

In response to efforts to censor songs like "Turbo Lover," the band recorded "Parental Guidance," which, according to Glen Tipton, "tells the parents of the world to leave their kids alone. . . . We've had enough of groups of mothers telling their kids what they should or should not listen to."[39] Underscoring the point, Halford says, "I know for a fact that rock's got all the elements of rebellion against your mom and dad. You want to stay up late, want to party all night long, you don't want to do your homework."[40]

Judas Priest has been accused of flirting with the occult and satanism. Certainly such album titles as *Sin After Sin* and *Defenders of the Faith* give credence to these charges.

KISS

With Kabuki-whitened faces and leather costumes, they appeared on stage puking blood, declaring, "God of rock 'n' roll, we'll steal your virgin soul." Producer Bob Ezrin described KISS as "symbols of unfettered evil and sensuality."[41] Their flair for stage violence earned the group a fanatical following, referred to as their "army." Rock magazines called them "fire-breathing demons from rock 'n' roll hell." Gene Simmons became known for his ability to lasciviously extend his tongue. On the liner notes for one album jacket, Simmons described his love techniques of "deliciously painful things that make you writhe and groan in ecstasy."[42] The album *Love Gun* contained a song dedicated to "Plaster Casters," rock music groupies who make plaster of paris replicas of famous rock stars' genitals.

Simmons says, "Marriage is not for me. I think it's natural for man to be promiscuous, and I think any muscle you don't exercise becomes dormant."[43] "We've always been committed to warping those little minds out there who get drivel on TV, like 'Father Knows Best,' and think that's what home life is all about."[44]

Not satisfied with their erotic image, band members evoked more satanic overtones. Former band member Peter Criss boldly declared, "I find myself evil. I believe in the devil as much as God. You can use either one to get things done."[45] Gene Simmons once confessed an interest in cannibalism and said, "If God is hot stuff, why is He afraid to have other gods before Him? I've always wanted to be God."[46]

KISS has had little respect for parents or anyone else concerned with morals. Simmons says, "The stage is the place where everything goes. It's the legal zone for flashers. . . . Nothing is sacred in rock 'n' roll. There's nothing that can't be done or shouldn't be done."[47] The

1987 album title *Crazy Nights* seems to sum up the group's ideology.

The group has removed its makeup but has maintained its large audiences. KISS has already sold $60 million in records, proof that evil and sensuality do sell and that the youth of America are willing to support raunchiness. Of their 1988 tour, Simmons said, "KISS fans are always there for us – and we're always there for them."[48] Small consolation for concerned parents.

KROKUS

Krokus is a Swiss heavy metal band whose main interest seems to be American women's sexuality. Mark Storace of the group says, "Girls in your country have the right idea when it comes to dealing with musicians. They just want to have a good time and not worry about lasting relationships."[49] In their song, "Long Stick Goes Boom," the singer says, "Let's do it right on the spot."

Their album entitled *One Vice at a Time* features an ad showing a number of vices listed, including depravity, lechery, sadism, voyeurism, fetishism, blasphemy, satanism, self-abuse, drunkenness, and misogyny. The ad says, "If rock 'n' roll is the ultimate vice, Krokus are prime offenders. Their latest example of excessive misconduct contains the most malicious, hard rock havoc."

Storace says, "When we're on the road, having sex is one of the things that keeps us going."[50] Storace adds, "Rock 'n' roll has always been a very sexual form, and Krokus, after all, is a rock 'n' roll band."[51]

MADONNA

Born the third child of eight in an Italian Catholic family, Madonna Louise Veronica Ciccone Penn became to the 1980s what Marilyn Monroe was to the 1950s. She said of herself, "I've been called a tramp, a harlot, a slut, and the kind of girl that always ends up in the backseat of a car."[52]

Nude photos appeared in *Penthouse* magazine, and she once starred in an underground pornographic film. When an English rock magazine inquired if it was difficult to lose her virginity, Madonna replied, "No. I thought of it as a career move."[53] Explaining why she had posed nude earlier in her career, she said, "You get paid $10 an hour versus $1.50 at Burger King."[54]

Rolling Stone said of her, "Like Prince, she recognized the virtue of a one-word name and demonstrated the truth of an old adage – sex sells. She has played America's public morals like a virtuoso, building her starlet to mega-slut to bad girl with a heart of gold to new honest woman."[55]

No female artist before her had ever whipped up such an erotic frenzy, dancing like Elvis Presley and looking like a younger, more voluptuous Mae West. Young women idolized her. One female fan said, "Madonna's living out our fantasies. She's able to do something our parents would never let us get away with."[56]

Madonna formerly wore a crucifix around her neck, see-through blouses, and fingerless gloves. She admitted the crucifix was because of her affinity for "a sexy man on a cross." But religious assertions aside, songs like "Burning Up" describe her on her knees willing to do anything as she says, "I have no shame." With her pouty, sex-kitten put-on, fans expected her fame to be short-lived, but a string of Top Ten hits gave Madonna hope for the future.

JOHN COUGAR MELLENCAMP

It's a long way from sadomasochism to patriotism, but John Cougar Mellencamp covers that entire lyrical spectrum. One of his earliest hits was "Hurts So Good," in which he invited his lover to sink her teeth into his bones and make it "hurt so good." Three years later he endeared himself to the nation with his sweet, nostalgic "Small Town."

After experiencing the altruism of Live Aid, John Cougar Mellencamp departed from some of his earlier, more rebellious attitudes. Several years ago during a London, Ontario, concert in front of 14,000 fans, he launched into an obscenity-laced tirade against the concert's promoters, flung rented equipment into the packed audience, allegedly injuring two women, and walked offstage.[57]

Mellencamp declared, "I swear because I know it's not socially acceptable, so I do it around people I know are going to be upset.

I hate things that are this-is-the-way-you-are-supposed-to-be-behave. That's why I hate schools, governments, and churches."[58] His popular "Jack and Diane" was an anthem of youthful rebellion. The "Authority Song" was in the same vein, though both songs lacked the viciousness of many of the anti-authority songs of heavy metal groups.

When criticized for the video "Hurts So Good" showing women in chains, Mellencamp said, "Sex, violence, rebellion–it's all part of rock 'n' roll."[59] Now, with his tune "Small Town" joining "Pink Houses" as populist anthems, Mellencamp says, "I've never voted, I've never registered to vote, but I will this time."[60] His 1987 album *The Lonesome Jubilee* showed that some mellowing had occurred.

MOTLEY CRUE

Their first commercial hit album featured a black front emblazoned with a satanic pentagram. It was entitled *Shout at the Devil*. Critics accused them of devilish overtones. Bass player Nikki Sixx defended the group by saying, "We're about as anti-Satan as you can get. We're trying to say that the devil is any authority who tells you what you can do and what you can't do. It can be your parents, it can be your teachers, it can be your boss. We're saying shout at the f——. Don't let them get you down!"[61]

Critics were even more alarmed when Sixx said, "We're the loudest, grossest band in the history of rock 'n' roll. Motley Crue isn't just a name. It's an image, and we do our damnedest to live up to it at all times."[62]

Tunes like "Red Hot" describe "love from a shotgun, licensed to kill." Another tune called "Bastard" extols the virtues of oral sex. Crue's lipstick and war paint, outrageously long hair-styles, knee boots, and skinny top-to-bottom black leather and studs appeals to heavy metal fans. Their tour bus features a sex room in the back, outfitted to show pornographic video-tapes. An article in a rock periodical claimed they took one young woman onto the bus and inflicted sadomasochistic sex acts upon her. Sixx says, "We treat women like s——. We're not Boy Scouts."

Their album *Theater of Pain* contained songs like "City Boy Blues," in which the singer says, "Don't look to Jesus to change your seasons." In the tune "Fight for Your Rights" the singer asks, "Who wrote the Bible?" He adds, "Save our souls for a life so good it sure feels bad." Nikki Sixx stated, "We're the nastiest, sleaziest band that's ever come down the pike, and we're proud of that. We have no intentions of changing."[63]

The band took a year-long break in 1986 but came back to record the album *Girls, Girls, Girls,* a tribute to the band's fondness for strip clubs. Describing the album, Nikki Sixx said, "It's VD rock–it's raunchier than anything we've ever done. Our attitude this time is just to pull your pants down and party."[64] Not too surprising, considering Sixx's later comment, "I've always done exactly what I wanted–not what people expected me to do."[65]

STEVIE NICKS

Fleetwood Mac was one of the top rock acts of the late 1970s. Members Lindsey Buckingham, Christine McVie, and Stevie Nicks pursued solo careers, but the group reunited for the 1987 album *Tango in the Night*. Stevie Nicks has also ventured into intense exploration of the occult.

Stevie admits believing in spirits, confesses that Halloween is her favorite night of the year, dabbles in reincarnation philosophy, wants to talk to a ghost, and expresses a desire to build her own pyramid and live in a witch-house.

The idea for the cover of her solo album *Bella Donna* came to her in a dream. It features a crystal ball (endorsing divination), a tambourine (symbolizing the porthole of perception to the spirit world), and three roses (representing the power of pyramids).[66] No wonder *Rolling Stone* called her "Fleetwood Mac's blond priestess of the occult."[67]

TED NUGENT

Billing himself as "the guitar gunslinger" and the Motor City Madman, Ted Nugent calls his music "combat rock," which involves a barrage of feedback and stage acrobatics, including Nugent's leap from atop amplifiers clad only in a loincloth. His pornographic lyrics are accompanied by guitar riffs amplified beyond the threshold of pain. Describing his outlook on rock, he declares, "Rock is a perfect primal method of releasing our violent instincts. I used to rape [an audience]. Now I like a little foreplay. I literally demand a reaction from an audience."[68] He apparently gets what he wants. His 1988 album *If You Can't Lick 'Em, Lick 'Em* featured a fatigued, sweaty female boxer on the cover, her legs spread wide. The album featured the title tune, plus, among others, "The Harder They Come, The Harder I Get."

OZZY OSBOURNE

After a decade of service to Black Sabbath, Ozzy Osbourne, the diabolical former lead singer for England's heavy metal Satan-rockers, is on his own. Lest anyone think that his split with Sabbath bodes good, Ozzy warns, "I'm just as evil and just as crazy as ever."[69]

No one who was there when he bit the head off a live dove at a CBS executive meeting would doubt him. "I wanted them to remember me," he explains, describing how he spat the remains on the table.[70] There's a lot to remember about Ozzy. Though he acknowledges the Satan-worshiping image in Sabbath's early days was a marketing ploy, he clings to his fascination with Lucifer. He professes a belief in future and past existences, one of which was lived as a "servant of the devil."[71] He is fascinated with Aleister Crowley, the famous British spiritualist, whom Ozzy calls "a phenomenon of his time."[72]

Drugs seemed as much a part of his life as the devil. He admits taking LSD every day for years, spending a thousand dollars a week on dope, snorting cocaine "by the bagful, and sampling heroin."[73]

His album *Diary of a Madman* was promoted by a $2 million concert tour featuring special effects and macabre props, including gallons of pig's blood.[74] A printed release enclosed with the LP publicized Ozzy's feelings: "I have become infatuated with the feeling of horror. . . . If my ideas seem disordered in intellect or slightly psychotic . . . it is because they are."

His album *Speak of the Devil* featured a fanged Ozzy vomiting simulated human flesh. *Speak of the Devil* included an earlier Black Sabbath tune praising marijuana entitled "Sweet Leaf." The album *Diary of a Madman* featured inverted crosses and black magic hieroglyphics. The tune "Little Dolls" spoke of voodoo. After biting the head off a bat and urinating on the Alamo, fans wondered what might come next. Pig intestines and calf livers were thrown into the audience.

PINK FLOYD

With forty-foot helium-inflated pigs floating in the air, a fusillade of fireworks, the amplified sounds of someone walking on the ceiling, a 35 by 210 foot cardboard wall rising from the stage, Pink Floyd concerts were rock theater at its best–or worst, depending on one's perspective. Their avant-garde sounds, propelled by the sale of 6.5 million units of their 1973 release *Dark Side of the Moon*, blitzed drug-doped audiences with high-tech space-rock sound.

One album, *The Wall*, earned Pink Floyd an amazing $20 million in one year by topping the charts week after week. *The Wall* chronicled the emotional torment of a successful rock star (Roger Waters, writer of the lyrics and music) who builds up a "wall" of defenses against an absent father, a smothering mother, and a sadistic schoolmaster.

The Wall lyrics explored psychic powers ("Nobody Home"), sex ("Young Lust—I need a dirty woman"), and educational anarchism. In "Another Brick in the Wall," Pink Floyd caustically intones that youth "don't need no education" or "thought control." What high school teacher could cope with students who heeded the plea: "Hey, teacher, leave them kids alone!"?

Rumors of the group's breakup abounded, but they released the album *A Momentary Lapse of Reason* in 1987.

PRINCE

Called Prince after his father's stage name, his full name is Prince Rogers Nelson. One of the more talented and versatile black musicians ever to enter pop music, he initially appealed to homosexuals with a scantily-clad image and lyrics endorsing incest and homosexual oral sex.

His tune "Darling Nikki" stirred a national protest over pornographic lyrics. It described a nymphomaniacal girl sitting in a hotel lobby "masturbating with a magazine." In the tune "Head," he told of a bride who meets him on her way to be wed. She engages in oral sex to preserve her virginity. *Rolling Stone* magazine described his quest for fame as a belief in "humanism through hedonism, social freedom through sexual anarchy."[75] Stage antics included simulated intercourse in a bed and a shower in a tub. The successful movie *Purple Rain* ended with Prince stroking the neck of his guitar, simulating masturbation until seminal fluid squirted from its end.

All of his albums contain liner notes giving thanks to God, but *People* magazine observed, "The gospel he preaches is salvation by sex."[76] His religious themes include a line from the tune "Darling Nikki"–"I'm fine because the Lord is coming soon." He admits his father beat his mother, who kept pornographic books and sexual vibrators in her room.[77] Prince shuns liquor and drugs and once left an open Bible in a band member's hotel room with a Scripture noted. One periodical said of him, "On stage he was the erotic Pope of Pop, possessed by his passion play . . . he'd wail in falsetto and perform coital contortions with a brass bed when necessary. Comparing Michael Jackson to Prince is like comparing Peter Pan with the Marquis de Sade."[78]

Prince's song "Sexuality" declares that a second coming, a "New-Age revolution," is on the horizon, an era when "anything goes." Where would Prince go next? His self-indulgent movie *Under the Cherry Moon* bombed, although his video for the tune "Kiss," showing Prince simulating copulation, was an instant success. His 1987 album *Sign o' the Times* shot to the top of the charts using his proven formula of eroticism and religion. He was shown nude on the cover of the 1988 album *Lovesexy.*

RATT

Ratt described their concert series as a "world infestation tour," an apt image for this Los Angeles-based quintet. An early album featured a dozen live rats crawling up a girl's leg. An advertisement for the album *Out of the Cellar* declared, "They're out of the cellar and out to conquer the earth." Stephen Pearcy of the group says, "We like sex, and we like getting loose after a show."[79]

The destination sign above the windshield of their travel bus invites women to expose their breasts. One magazine described their touring vehicle as a "rolling Sodom and Gomorrah," a "nightmare vision of rock depravity."[80] The 1985 album title *Invasion of Your Privacy* seems appropriate for this group.

Robbin Crosby of the band says, "I don't have a love life, I have a lust life."[81] The hedonist hymns "Sweet Cheater" and "Back for More" bear lyrical testimony to Ratt's intentions. The video for "Lay It Down" suggests prepubescent sex between two youngsters at a birthday party. Their libidinous lyrics are matched by the devotion of their fans, postpubescents whose attention spans seem limited to the hormonal moment and who frequently throw panties and bras on stage.

THE ROLLING STONES

Their early image of savagery, evil, and rebellion is intact, thanks to Keith Richards's heroin bust and Mick Jagger's promiscuous meanderings. Richards admits, "There are black magicians who think we are acting as unknown agents of Lucifer."[82] To support such speculation, the Stones' songs have ranged from supporting violent revolution in "Street Fighting Man" to the satanists' anthem "Sympathy for the Devil." The death of four fans at the fateful Altamont rockfest solidified their image as purveyors of the sinister.

A Stones concert is an orgy of sexual celebration, with Jagger as head cheerleader. Strutting and prancing across the stage, his androgynous performances delight both men and women. On one tour, his playacting concluded with a giant phallic balloon rising out of the stage. "Sometimes, being on stage is better than an orgasm," Jagger claims.[83] Press reports circulate regularly that Jagger is bisexual.

Today's band members average more than forty years of age, and Bill Wyman is over fifty. Showing no signs of mellowing, the Stones' tune "She Was Hot" describes a singer lost in a woman's "burning flesh" as she "pinned me to the ground." The tune "Too Much Blood" describes a man cutting off a woman's head, putting her body in a refrigerator, and then features the singer yelling sexual expletives.

Commenting on his promiscuity and infidelity to his live-in lover, Jerri Hall, Mick Jagger said, "I've told Jerri I can't feel cut off from half the population."[84] (Jagger did eventually marry Hall.)

As he and the other Stones continue to rock on (their 1981 tour grossed an estimated $127 million, including $300,000 a day on T-shirt sales alone), Jagger's sadomasochistic view of women lingers with salacious lines like, "When the whip comes down," and "Am I rough enough?" (from "Beast of Burden").

No one knows the future of the Stones. Rumors of a break-up abound, as they have for years. But even when the Stones have disbanded, their legacy of sensuality and Satanism will continue for years.

SCORPIONS

The first German heavy metal band to gain worldwide recognition, the Scorpions called themselves "virgin killers." The album with that name showed the photo of a naked ten-year-old girl sitting on shards of jagged glass, her legs spread open and arrows pointing to her genitals. Their big Top 40 hit was entitled, "Rock You Like a Hurricane." The singer says his lover is hungry, so he is going to "give her inches and feed her well."

Klaus Meine of the band says the song is autobiographical. "It's strange waking up in some strange city with a new girl lying next to you every day, but it's something we've gotten used to," Mien declares.[85] Complaints were registered about the album *Love at First Sting* from which the tune "Rock You like a Hurricane" was taken. The cover depicted a partially clad couple embracing, as the man tattooed a scorpion on the woman's thigh. More offensive was the cover for the album *Black Out,* which showed a lobotomy patient whose eyes were being clawed out by bent forks. The album *Animal Magnetism* pictured a woman kneeling in front of a man's legs as a Doberman pinscher thrust out its tongue.[86] In response to cries of protest, a member of the band said, "It was a sensual cover . . . rock 'n' roll is a very sensual form, and we're a very sensual band."[87] The 1988 album *Savage Amusement* proved that the band had not changed its image.

TWISTED SISTER

"I'm a dirtbag, and I'm not ashamed of it," says lead singer Dee Snyder of Twisted Sister.[88] When the group first started performing, band members wore dresses on stage to get attention. Snyder says, "Our philosophy has always been to do anything to become famous."[89]

The lyrics to "We're Not Gonna Take It Anymore" foster rebellion. The video accompanying the tune features a dictatorial father who doesn't want his son playing the guitar to a Twisted Sister record. The opening chords of the song literally blow the boy's father through the window.

The video for the song "I Want to Rock" is set in a school where a boy chases his tyrannical teacher through the school until the instructor gets blown up. On the cover to their introductory album *Stay Hungry,* Dee Snyder holds what appears to be a human shank bone with flesh drooping from it.

After the obscurity of a Long Island rock club, Snyder now has the attention of the popular press and says of the music he plays, "Heavy metal is the only form of music other than punk that has retained the basic elements of rock 'n' roll—rebellion."[90] Asked about how he prepares for a concert, Dee Snyder said, "I think about things I hate."[91] Appropriate for such a group, their 1987 album was titled *Love Is for Suckers*.

VAN HALEN/DAVID LEE ROTH

When a rock band describes itself as "a group of barbarians who are sweeping around the world," it's obvious their goals transcend mere musical performance.[92] Former lead singer David Lee Roth confessed, "I've managed to live out 100 percent of my fantasies with pretty women I've met on the road."[93] Gesturing with the microphone as an erect phallus between his legs, he added, "We celebrate all the sex and violence of television . . . that's Van Halen."[94] Roth's rampant sexuality made the band famous with tunes like "Hot for the Teacher," describing lustful abandon. Other tunes like "House of Pain" zeroed in on sadomasochism.

Roth has been quoted as saying, "We've indulged in every possible vice that can be counted on the road."[95] He also says, "I admire and respect women. They know their place—under me."[96]

One concert critic described a Van Halen performance this way: "Van Halen in concert is a musical circus of sex, drugs, and rock 'n' roll clichés piled on so thick it might take the form of high camp were it not for the screaming fans devouring every exaggerated pose. Sex is celebrated in a way that makes bike gangs look like morality squads."[97]

With the addition of new lead singer Sammy Hagar, Van Halen's popularity continued. Roth was only a quarter of the group, which includes bass guitarist Michael Anthony, and the Dutch-born Van Halen brothers, Edward and Alex. Edward declares, "I'm in rock 'n' roll because I don't like being told what to do."[98] But Roth's high-leaping, crotch-thrusting antics defined the group's philosophy beyond realistic doubt. He proclaimed, "Whatever your vice, whatever your sexual ideas . . . whatever somebody else can't do in his nine-to-five job, I can do in rock and roll. . . . I'm in the job to exercise my sexual fantasies. When I'm onstage, it's like doing it with 20,000 of your closest friends. . . . I'm proud of the way we live."[99] His 1988 album *Skyscraper* featured the song "Hot Dog and a Shake" and other ventures into thinly disguised rock porn.

WASP

"I'm a liar and I'm a cheat, I have no morals and I'm a thief, I'm a tormentor, I'm a sadist that whips the flesh."

Those words from the song "Tormentor" are an apt description of WASP bandleader Blackie

Lawless. The band's acronym stands for "We Are Sexual Perverts."[100] Song titles run the gamut from "The Torture Never Stops" and "Love Machine" to "On Your Knees," an overt description of oral sex.

WASP's early stage shows featured naked women on torture racks, whips, raw meat thrown into the audience, and blood drunk from a skull. Such antics were eventually discarded in favor of a Lawless costume with holes in the back of his pants and a buzz saw jutting from a codpiece on his crotch. Explaining such stage tactics, Lawless said, "We knew that we'd have to be totally off the wall in our appearance and sound for anyone to give us a second look."[101] With abandoned bluntness, Lawless says, "If I wasn't in WASP, I'd be out stealing cars."[102]

Later stage shows did away with the psychodramatic trappings but not the sexually explicit lyrics, as evidenced in tunes like "Ball Crusher" and "Sex Drive." The cover for the single record "Ball Crusher" shows a girl with her hand coming out of a guy's pants and holding a bloody baseball. Lawless says about attempts to censor his songs, "I don't see anything wrong with sex and violence, as long as violence is presented in a very theatrical way. It's very therapeutic for kids."[103]

The band's 1986 album *Inside the Electric Circus* featured a cover with Lawless poised behind cage bars, clad in tigerlike stripes that had been painted on his body. Like many contemporary bands, WASP seems determined to exploit man's animal nature. Appropriately, the 1987 album was titled *Live . . . Animal*.

WHITESNAKE

David Coverdale, formerly with Deep Purple, heads this British heavy metal group that has just recently made it big in the U.S. While Coverdale has taken a strong stand against drugs, he is just as firm in his insistence that rock is sexual. Whitesnake's album titles *Love Hunter* and *Slide It In* (showing a snake crawling into a woman's cleavage) proclaim the group's basic message. The group's videos bring that message with shocking directness into American living rooms. Coverdale's girlfriend has been featured in the group's salacious videos.

Whitesnake's album covers have a subdued, polished look compared with most heavy metal album covers. The single "Still of the Night" was popular outside heavy metal circles. In fact, Whitesnake seems to present a more sophisticated view of sex than, say, adolescent-style head-bangers Motley Crue or AC/DC, but despite looking older and wiser, they still focus on sex-as-fulfillment. In a 1988 interview, Coverdale stated, "I have all the regard in the world for our audiences. . . . I believe that they, too, are aware of my respect and dignity."[104] One wonders what sort of respect and dignity are possible in romantic relationships based on the kind of sexuality seen in Whitesnake's videos and lyrics.

CHAPTER

4

Now That I Know, What Do I Do?

After reading this far, you should be convinced that much of the rock scene is morally questionable and filled with perversion and debauchery. You're probably thinking, *How could my children tolerate such filth saturating their minds day after day?* Think *peer pressure.*

It would be an eye-opener to spend a day at your children's school and listen to their friends' discussions. Because most students know the words and melodies of every hit on the charts, imagine how your children would feel if they didn't. It's understood in youth culture: *Everybody* listens to rock. Your children couldn't communicate with their peers if they were unaware of Prince's latest album, David Lee Roth's most recent paramour, and the much-publicized drug bust of their favorite group.

Your son puts on his tattered blue jeans, dons his metal-studded leather jacket, and leaves for a concert looking like a replica of the other ten thousand kids there. You can see right through the conformity of his so-called nonconformity, but he can't.

You need acceptance as much as your children do. Where do you get acceptance? From social clubs, business associates, organized institutions, and, most of all, your spouse. None of these options are readily available to teenagers.

In addition, youth face sexual pressures every day. Advertisers convey the message that we must work for attraction from the opposite sex. Put yourself in your children's position. If they violate the norm of being tuned in and turned on to the world of rock, what potential partners would look at them?

So what can a parent do? Be sympathetic to the problems and pressures of youth. Concentrate on your own children. They may fight with you, but underneath they know you're doing what you think is best. You don't have to know every song and singer on the charts to point out the obvious spiritual deficiencies in their lives and to question your children's identification with their life-styles.

Suppose your children are caught up in the rock culture. Don't release your frustrations in anger. Should you burn your son's Black Sabbath T-shirt and insist he break all his rock albums? You can, but the cure might be worse than the cause.

Four things can help you communicate with your children about the negative aspects of rock:

1. Be informed.
2. Show love.
3. Set an example.
4. Provide alternatives.

More Help for Parents

Additional resources on rock music are available from the following:

Bob Larson Ministries
P.O. Box 36A
Denver, CO 80236
(303) 980-1511

Al Menconi Ministries
Box 969
Cardiff by the Sea, CA 92007
(619) 436-8676

Peters Brothers
Box 9222
N. St. Paul, MN 55109
(612) 770-8114

STEP ONE: BE INFORMED

It's surprising how little most parents know about the world of music their children live in. I have waited outside rock concerts and watched cars disgorging teenage occupants. "Have a good time," Mom says as she drives away, dumping her thirteen-year-old daughter into a pot-hazed evening of drugs and titillating sexual innuendo.

Many rock concerts are free zones of drug usage. The atmosphere is so saturated with euphoric odors that one deep breath is nearly enough to get high. Before the first song is played, joints light up. Those who don't come supplied with their own bag full of goodies can easily borrow from a friend. The band onstage exhorts the crowd, "Get high and groove with the sounds."

Police react with indifference. To arrest drug offenders would start a riot with serious injuries, and what can be done with five thousand kids after you've arrested them?

Why don't more parents know what's going on? Would some parents rather ignore the truth?

I was once scolded by a woman for displaying shocking album covers in my lecture at a church. She later apologized to me when she found the same kind of covers in her son's record collection. Then she told me how she coped with the situation.

"I asked him to go through each album with me and tell me something about each group. At first, he was reluctant. I guess he thought I only wanted to condemn, but after a while he opened up and showed me the lyric sheets. Reading those words was quite a jolt."

She went on. "I did my best not to react self-righteously and, instead, put the burden back on him. I asked questions like, 'Do you really think it's wise to fill your mind with that outlook on life?' "

Instead of condemning her son's musical tastes, this mother tried to understand his world without being judgmental. She had every reason for concern about the spiritual consequences of his music, but she honestly admitted that her ignorance and oversight had allowed him to purchase those albums in the first place.

"Finally," she continued, "I asked him to play some of the albums for me. I told him not to spare me and pick the worst record he had. He chose Motley Crue. By the time they got through describing quickie sex on an elevator, I thought I'd be sick. By the look on my son's face, he wasn't so sure he liked the words either."

"The turning point came," she concluded, "when I confessed to him my failings as a parent. He had never heard that kind of admission from me before. I left his room knowing for the first time I understood a little about the influences in my son's life. He didn't get rid of those records on the spot. That might have been too much to expect. What's more important is that once again I'm talking with my son."

STEP TWO: SHOW LOVE

When was the last time you verbalized affection to your child? You feel it, so why don't you look at your child and say, "I love you"?

My counseling experiences indicate that verbal expressions of love in most homes are sporadic. "I love you" is hard to say because those three words must be based on frequent, open communication. Otherwise, the words are forced and shallow.

While counseling teenagers, I often asked this question: "If you had serious personal problems, to whom would you go for advice?"

The list of prospects included friends, school counselors, clergy, even casual acquaintances. In fact, teenagers discussed with me things they have never told their parents. That's tragic. Parents should be the first resort in times of need. Their counsel should be sought constantly.

Why don't parents top the list? Moms and dads should ask themselves these questions:

- Am I too busy to spend time with my children?
- Am I aware of what's going on in their world?
- Can they talk freely with me about anything at any time?
- Do they know that I really love them, and do I tell them so?

If your answer to any of these questions is no, you have some clues about the lack of communication with your child. Stop for a moment and listen to the songs they're hearing. Their rock heroes are saying, "We understand your problems. Get high with us. We've got the answers."

Though false, they hear that message all day long and are convinced of its veracity. Your child may know deep inside that you love him and care about his welfare. But unless you tell him what you feel, it won't do much good.

This is a plea for something that is going out of style–family togetherness. Why do families spend so little time together? Most families congregate only to eat or watch television. Mealtime is hardly an effective open forum, since in many homes it's hurry-up time. And viewing television is not conducive to getting to know each other.

What about this suggestion? Spend your next weekend with the family–just them!

A Case Study: Family Lessons in Loving

I should have known the moment we got in the car that I was in for it. The teenager driving me to a Sunday luncheon engagement turned the radio to his favorite rock station. It was blaring at full volume the heaviest sounds he could find. We were headed for his parent's home, and the worst was yet to come.

The feast set before us was worthy of a king. The atmosphere at the dinner table was slightly tense, but I dismissed it as apprehension about having a new guest at dinner.

I was wrong. It soon became obvious this meal had been arranged to resolve a longstanding parent-child confrontation. About halfway through the meal, the mother folded her arms.

"Mr. Larson," she began, her formal tone exposing her real intentions, "don't you think that when parents tell their children not to listen to certain kinds of music, they should obey?"

Her teenage son slowly slid down in his chair. He knew it was coming, but the question still embarrassed him.

I paused for what must have seemed an eternity to both of them.

"Please answer a question for me first," I finally replied. "Do you love your son?"

She was stunned—and offended.

"What do you mean?" she asked. "I brought him into the world, didn't I? I cook his meals and provide for him."

"You're not answering my question," I insisted.

Gradually, the intent of my inquiry hit home. Her body relaxed, and she hung her head.

"Yes," she answered. "I do love my son."

"Well, then," I probed further, "when was the last time you told him?"

Tears welled in her eyes. She had invited me there to put her son on the spot. Instead, she was in the hot seat.

I glanced at her son, who barely suppressed his glee at seeing Mom on the defensive for a change.

"Do you love your parents?" I asked him.

The boy hung his head. He didn't enjoy having the shoe on his own foot.

I barely heard the yes he muttered under his breath, but his answer was audible enough to warrant my next question.

"When was the last time you told them?"

He looked across the table at his parents. Almost simultaneously, the three of them burst into tears.

Before leaving, we all joined hands around the table for a time of prayer to heal the scars of a wounded home.

Cancel all other plans. Leave the television and stereo off and get acquainted with the people who love you most. If your kids carry their Walkmans with them, fine. If you engage them in heart-to-heart conversation enough, they may find that they can do without the Walkman for a while.

STEP THREE: SET AN EXAMPLE

Perhaps you've tried to discipline your child's musical habits, but he just won't listen. Could your failure stem from a lack of moral authority? Do you contradict yourself?

One reason children ignore instructions regarding musical standards is parental inconsistency. Adult hypocrisy can help turn kids off to Mom and Dad and on to Billy Idol.

Whenever I challenge teenagers to use discrimination regarding choosing popular music, they immediately present two arguments: "What about the TV programs my parents watch?" and "Their music isn't much better."

What about it, Mom and Dad? Is your example an asset or a detriment? Can you be honest with yourselves and your children? Let's examine some adult hypocrisies that drive teenagers deeper into the rock culture. *Television*. As you consider your child propagandized by Prince, he sees you as brainwashed by "Falcon Crest" and "Dallas"–or by the sexier fare on cable.

This is not the place for a tirade against all TV programs, since a few are creative and genuinely entertaining.

But consider that great American institution, the soap opera, which has come to exemplify the immorality of TV:

1. *The life-styles presented as normal are concoctions of writers who foist their moral foibles on the American housewife.*

In the typical soap household, women are wicked and men are manipulative. Do you yearn to cheat on your husband, suspect him of sleeping with his secretary, expect to have your teenage daughter turn up pregnant, and plan to slit your wrists in the throes of mental depression? If so, the soaps adequately represent your life. If not, then why subject your family to immoral drama?

2. *Viewers are coerced into identifying with soap characters.*

Viewers cry, laugh, and indulge each emotional trauma as if the actors were real people. Such empathizing may cause you to rationalize sin, sympathizing with the harried wife who seeks solace in seduction. *After all,* you might think, *that tormenting husband drove her to it.*

3. *What you see on television may not seem as repulsive in real life once you have been thoroughly indoctrinated.*

Soaps set trends for America's moral attitude toward life and love. And what's true for the soaps is true for prime-time programs, too.

Music. Most adults are stunned when they learn the lyrics of the rock tunes their children listen to. Why have they never noticed the words of their favorite songs?

For example, triangle-affair songs and casual adultery lubricated with liquor provide the main subject matter of country and western

What's Your TV Intake?

Try this experiment. For one week's average viewing schedule, make a list of how many times you are subjected to the following:

- adultery and fornication portrayed or suggested
- murders or attempted murders
- verbal and physical assaults
- favorable attitudes toward homosexuality
- cheating and corner-cutting to get ahead
- profanity
- dirty jokes and lewd remarks
- the Lord's name used in vain
- Christianity mocked or attacked
- occult practices glorified or used to instill horror.

The completed list may appall you, but show it to your child and tell him what you plan to do about it. (You will, I hope, decide to carefully monitor future viewing habits in your home). Ask your child to follow your example. Ask him to compile a similar list based on the music he listens to and the rock stars he admires.

music. Which is worse, AC/DC singing, "Lickin' off the sweat on her favorite trick" or Conway Twitty declaring, "We've never been this far before"? KISS may not be paragons of moral virtue, but are they much worse than erotically enhanced Dolly Parton?

Sex isn't country music's only subject. Topic number two is alcohol.

Songs praising booze include "Red Wine and Blue Memories," "Two More Bottles of Wine," "Whiskey Trip," "The Power of Positive Drinking," "Heaven Was a Drink of Wine," and "Bartender Blues."

Substance abuse is also a part of many singing stars' life-styles. Waylon Jennings admits he was seriously addicted to cocaine and claims that his album *Turn the Page* was the first record in twenty years he recorded without the assistance of drugs. Willie Nelson caused a controversy during the Carter presidency when he and his band, invited to perform at the White House, told reporters that the band did *not* perform unless they had smoked pot first.

STEP FOUR: PROVIDE ALTERNATIVES

"But there's nothing else to listen to!"

That defense is typical after suggesting that a young person diminish his steady diet of rock music. He has never learned to understand other kinds of music, and his artistic appreciation is stunted. Taking away rock removes an emotional security blanket that leaves some teenage lives in a musical vacuum. The fact may be painful, but true: *Your kids are determined to have rock music in their lives.*

Most teens have little interest in the classics and are bored by the middle-of-the-road pop sounds. But they crave rock. It's part of their upbringing, and the thought of going through

Your Life-Style and Drugs

Kids are always watching their parents, and they notice when Mom and Dad use alcohol, muscle relaxers, or tranquilizers to cope with stress. It is unlikely that you are using any illegal substances, but do you ever find that chemicals help you "unwind" or face a stressful situation? You can be sure your child has noticed.

An occasional use of a prescribed muscle relaxer is no crime, but be aware that our whole culture is oriented toward seeking pleasure and avoiding pain. If your own habits convey the message that drugs are useful for coping with stress and making life more pleasant, you are helping your child toward drug use. Cocaine may be a far cry from a once-a-week Valium, but the best thing you can do in your home is to show that mature people can have a good time—and cope with the bad times—without resorting to drugs and alcohol.

life without sound and rhythm is a dismal prospect.

There is a simple answer. Show young people there is something else to listen to, music that speaks to them in an acceptable, enjoyable idiom. Contemporary Christian music has experienced a dramatic upheaval resulting in a diversity of recorded sounds to inspire faith, to minister to deep needs, and to simply enjoy.

Much Christian music today is both musically sophisticated and well-grounded theologically. Not all of it is good, of course, but there is a clear attempt by many artists to honor God while reaching teens.

Something else has happened. Records and tapes are the fastest growing aspect of the Christian bookseller industry. Many stores report that 50 percent of their sales volume is contemporary Christian music.

The airwaves are filled with it. In the United States, over 2,500 stations program some Christian music. Many Christian stations have devoted entire formats to contemporary sounds.

Christian music is big business. People like Amy Grant, Russ Taff, Petra, and Phil Keaggy—to mention a few—produce albums that compete commercially in the secular marketplace.

Young people who forsake the degenerate sounds of secular rock do have an option. Christian bookstores and many local record stores have stacks of albums by artists whose musical expression reflects youthful thinking *and* moral integrity.

Having said all this, I believe that we don't necessarily have to limit ourselves to Christian music. There are many rock artists whose lifestyles and lyrics are above reproach. While it isn't possible here to recommend individuals—so much can change by the time this book is in print—it is possible to encourage you to en-

Is Christian Rock Really Different?

Some of that Christian music doesn't sound any different from secular rock. So what good will it do to encourage your kids to buy contemporary Christian records?

The lyrics of the songs won't be saturated with immorality. The musicians have given their talents to the Lord. Most are genuinely concerned about honoring Jesus.

But the music is still the same—it's got that THUMP-THUMP beat.

A lot of the songs do. There are even Christian heavy metal bands (Stryper, for example), and their music—though not their lyrics—is as "heavy" as any secular group's. But this isn't typical of most contemporary Christian music.

Contemporary Christian music is young and growing. It has many shortcomings, and some inconsistencies are too apparent. But even the worst modern attempts at expressing Christian faith are better than the secular sex-drenched paeans to hedonism.

ter into your child's life and interests so that you can know what sort of records your children are buying.

Parenting in the 1990s is going to be complex, and maybe you think you won't have time to monitor every album or tape your child buys.

But try. Keep communication open so that you're welcome in your son or daughter's room. In an atmosphere of trust, your child won't mind your seeing his newest album, and you can feel free to discuss the cover and the lyrics. In close, loving families, you could even browse through the record stores with your child. He isn't likely to buy something offensive if you're there giving feedback.

NOTES

CHAPTER 1

1. *People,* November 1985.
2. *Billboard,* 29 June 1985, 10.
3. *Hit Parader,* 28 February 1986, 28.
4. *Hit Parader,* July 1986, 61.
5. *Time,* 30 September 1985, 70.
6. *Music News* (no date), 9-11, 15, 62, 64-66.
7. Ibid.
8. Parents Music Resource Center Letter, 300 Metropolitan Square, 655 15th St., N.W., Washington, DC 20005.

CHAPTER 2

1. *Hit Parader,* August 1984, 20-22.
2. *Circus,* 16 August 1976, 30.
3. *Circus,* 22 June 1978, 15.
4. *Circus,* 12 October 1976, 41.
5. *Rolling Stone* (no date).
6. *Billboard,* Heavy Metal Issue, 1985, 81.
7. *Hit Parader,* May 1985, 42.
8. *Hit Parader,* May 1987, 34.
9. *Billboard,* 6 July 1985, 22.
10. *Woman's World,* 2 April 1985, 6.
11. *USA Today,* 18 October 1986, 2D.
12. *Billboard,* 20 July 1985, 3.
13. *Time,* 26 December 1983, 56.
14. *Cleveland Plain Dealer,* 15 April 1984, 9D.
15. *Newsweek,* 30 December 1985, 54.

16. *Cleveland Plain Dealer,* 15 April 1984, 1D.
17. *Newsweek,* 30 December 1985, 56.
18. *U.S. News and World Report,* 28 October 1985, 49.
19. *USA Today,* 14 May 1986, 1D.

CHAPTER 3

1. *Circus,* 28 February 1986, 34.
2. Ibid., 35.
3. *Hit Parader,* June 1988, 44.
4. *Billboard,* 15 February 1986, 47.
5. *Hit Parader,* June 1988, 12.
6. *Hit Parader,* August 1986, 6.
7. *Hit Parader,* June 1985, 61.
8. *Washington Times,* 16 April 1986.
9. *Circus,* 30 November 1987, 57.
10. *Rolling Stone,* 12 January 1978, 13.
11. Ibid., 83.
12. *Newsweek,* 18 July 1983, 76.
13. Ibid., 57.
14. *Rolling Stone,* 11 February 1983, 43-45.
15. *Campus Life,* April 1984, 40.
16. *People,* 23 April 1984, 94.
17. *Rolling Stone,* 7 June 1984, 13.
18. *Hit Parader,* May 1987, 16.
19. Ibid.
20. *Hit Parader,* August 1983, 64.
21. *Rolling Stone,* 7 July 1983, 43.
22. *Billboard,* 24 September 1983, 38.
23. *Hit Parader,* November 1982, 61.
24. *Hit Parader,* February 1986, 9.
25. *Birmingham News,* 26 September 1985, 10D.
26. *People,* 12 July 1976, 50.
27. *USA Today,* 22 August 1984, 1D.
28. *Song Hits,* May 1984, 15.
29. *The Calgary Sun,* 27 June 1982, 42.
30. *Hit Parader,* June 1984, 4.
31. *Circus,* 31 January 1983, 42.
32. *Rolling Stone,* 17 October 1976, 17.
33. *Newsweek,* 27 February 1984, 51.
34. *Hit Parader,* September 1982, 25.
35. *Hit Parader,* Fall 1983, 58.

36. *Circus*, 31 July 1982, 52.
37. *Hit Parader*, June 1982, 5.
38. *Rolling Stone*, 15 September 1980, 14.
39. *Hit Parader*, May 1981, 69.
40. *Hit Parader*, February 1983, 59.
41. *Rolling Stone*, 25 March 1976, 9.
42. Ibid., 20.
43. *US*, 14 January 1985, 31.
44. Ibid., 30.
45. *Rolling Stone*, 7 April 1977, 49.
46. *Circus*, 13 September 1976, 42.
47. *Hit Parader*, June 1986, 13.
48. *Hit Parader*, June 1988, 18.
49. *Hit Parader*, July 1982, 41.
50. *Hit Parader*, February 1985, 57.
51. *Hit Parader*, May 1986, 55.
52. *People*, 11 March 1985, 113.
53. *Time*, 4 March 1985, 75.
54. *Rocky Mountain News*, 14 January 1985, 2G.
55. *Rolling Stone*, Summer 1986, 121.
56. *People*, 13 May 1985, 43.
57. *Rolling Stone*, 28 October 1982, 39.
58. *People*, 11 October 1982.
59. *Musician*, February 1983, 22.
60. *Rolling Stone* (no date), John Cougar Mellencamp interview.
61. *Hit Parader*, December 1983, 36-37.
62. Ibid.
63. *Hit Parader*, May 1985, 6.
64. *Hit Parader*, May 1987, 40.
65. *Hit Parader*, June 1988, 58.
66. *Rolling Stone*, 3 September 1981, 18.
67. *Rolling Stone*, 17 September 1981, 57.
68. *Circus*, 13 May 1976, 29.
69. *Hit Parader*, March 1981, 27.
70. *Rolling Stone*, 14 May 1981, 41.
71. *Circus*, 26 August 1980, 26.
72. Ibid.
73. *People*, 7 September 1981.
74. *Rolling Stone*, 12 November 1981, 39.
75. *Rolling Stone*, 9 December 1982, 67.
76. *People*, 19 November 1984, 161.

77. Ibid., 162.
78. *US,* 10 September 1984, 44.
79. *Hit Parader,* August 1985, 35.
80. *People,* 12 August 1985, 117-119.
81. *Circus,* 30 September 1985, 43-48.
82. *Rolling Stone,* 19 August 1971.
83. *Rolling Stone,* 17 July 1975, 37.
84. *People,* 3 October 1977, 108.
85. *Hit Parader,* May 1984, 21.
86. *Circus,* 31 October 1985, 56.
87. *Hit Parader,* January 1984, 6.
88. *Hit Parader,* March 1986, 37.
89. *Hit Parader,* January 1985, 65.
90. *Billboard,* 22 September 1984, 50.
91. *Rolling Stone,* 22 November 1984, 64.
92. *Circus,* 10 October 1978, 26.
93. *Circus,* 14 November 1979, 42.
94. *Circus,* 17 October 1978, 39.
95. *Hit Parader,* September 1982, 5.
96. *Hit Parader,* August 1985, 17.
97. *Calgary Herald,* 28 April 1984.
98. *Circus,* 13 May 1980, 23.
99. *Rolling Stone,* 4 September 1980, 9-10, 21.
100. *Circus,* 31 January 1985, 38.
101. *Hit Parader,* March 1985, 37.
102. *Hit Parader,* May 1987, 25.
103. *Hit Parader,* May 1986, 13.
104. *Hit Parader,* June 1988, 39.

About the Author

BOB LARSON is president of the International Broadcasting Network in Denver, Colorado. He has lectured in more than seventy countries on the subject of contemporary culture and is the author of *Larson's Book of Cults*, *Larson's Book of Rock*, and *Larson's Book of Family Issues*. He hosts a daily nationwide live radio talk show, "TALK-BACK with Bob Larson."